PHOTO BY GRAHAM HOLLEY

Edi Holley is an artist and writer who has written six books of stories and two short novels. She has also written a book of family memoirs and three poetry chapbooks. She reads on the New York Poetry Circuit. Holley has two children and lives in New York and New Hampshire.

ALSO BY EDI HOLLEY

JUST STORIES

THE STORY TELLER

MAINE STORIES

FIVE CHRISTMAS STORIES

CUP OF GOLD

BY LOVE HELD BOUND

NOR'EASTER

GOOCHE'S BEACH

HOOFS & PAWS

TAILS AND CLAWS

HONEY-LOVING WAYS

HONEY-LOVING WAYS

Story and Art

by

Edi Holley

White Barn Press
626 Pickering Rd.
Rochester, NH, 03867

Acknowledgements:

Cindy Hochman, *"100 Proof" Copyediting Services*

and for her life-giving encouragement

*and **Carol Masana**, my computer goddess*

HONEY-LOVING WAYS

I am looking through an amber stained-glass window composed of hexagonal shapes. I feel drenched in sunlight, in a bath of golden honey. I hear soft whirring sounds. Suddenly, into this dream comes a huge black paw striking through the liquid gold. I thought only the fairies knew there was a hive of precious honey in the hole in the old oak tree.

She snuffled and she snorted among the green undergrowth, smelling the grubs and delicious ants that she loved to slurp up on her tongue to get extra protein for the winter ahead.

But, what was that? She sniffed another smell …a sweet, delicious, irresistible, fabulissimo other smell of H O N E Y—her absolute favorite in the world—and so she let her nose lead her. Her huge body drifted along behind as she hurried through the woods, not even noticing the nasty wood fairies dancing around, occasionally twanging a twig in her face and pulling at her ears. She just kept on humming a growly little tune as she crashed through rotting logs and ferns until she saw a golden vision: a halo of bees flying in a cloud around a hive that reeked of the most delicious substance you could imagine—honey.

And there were the worker bees, flying with loads of flower nectar in their honey stomachs that they had gathered in the clover fields and were flying back to deposit in the comb. When they got there, the most amazing thing happened. The bee that brought a load of honey was doing a dance! And all the other bees had gathered 'round to watch her. It went like this:

You wiggle to the left
Then you waggle to the right
You do the hoobie doobie
with all your might.
Hoobie Doobie
Hoobie Doobie
Doo-Wah Doo-Wah Doo-Wah

The bee was waggling her abdomen and dancing up and down inside the nest. She turned to the left and turned to the right to make a figure eight. She was showing the others the distance to the nectar by the length of straight runs and by the number of waggles. The faster she waggled, the more nectar there was. She did the dance over and over again while the other bees watched. Then she gave the other bees a sip of the nectar through her long tongue so they knew by the smell which flowers to look for.

the pixies and fairies danced on Bertha's nose and darted in and out of her ears. They even pulled her stubby little tail until she growled and snapped at them, but, really, she was so intent on the honey that she hardly noticed them at all. She HAD to get the honey. It was like ice cream to her; for her, it was better than ice-cream. As soon as her nose told her she was close enough, she lunged headlong into the hive, flinging a great brown paw out to scoop it up.

It dripped all over her beautiful brown fur. Finally she managed to scoop out a mouthful of the delicious stuff—*mmmmmm*. THE BEES WERE AS MAD AS HORNETS. They buzzed and flew wildly around her head, stinging every MAD AS HORNETS. They buzzed and flew wildly around her head, stinging every spot they could find until they found her most sensitive spot ... her nose. And, with that, she let out the most awful hollering bear yell, which echoed throughout the woods so that the skunks and foxes and raccoons and rabbits went flying into their holes. And the hoot owl swiveled her head around and around and began to hoot and and hoot, so that even Pan, the great God of Nature came to see what the fuss was all about.

When the Magic Fairy heard the ruckus, she appeared in a blaze of light and said, "What's all this about?" The bees all buzzed so wildly, she couldn't hear what they were saying, so the head pixie, who had hopped on top of a mushroom, loudly answered, "This disgusting bear has ruined the hive and she's eating all the honey the bees have worked on all summer to save for winter."

"Get rid of her! Get rid of her," chimed in all the bees.

And, so, with a flick of the wrist, the Magic Fairy transformed Bertha. She just shriveled right down and became a tiny green snake, sliding in circles at the base of the giant mushroom, flickering her forked tongue out to taste the air, and looking very, very cross. Two pixies danced on the top of the mushroom in a lovely little pas de deux to celebrate, and all the bees clapped their wings and their six feet together. And out of the darkness of the deep woods they could see the eyes of all the wood creatures shining like flashlights, watching their dance.

Meanwhile, the Magic Fairy waved her wand over the hive so that the damage Bertha had done was gone, and the workers went about busily checking their beautiful hexagonal cells where they stored their honey. Everything had to be perfect for the worker bees.

But something new had happened. Now the workers had also built a few strange-looking cells along the outer edge of the honeycomb. They looked like rough peanut shells. The queen laid a very special tiny egg inside each one. After three days and three nights, an iggly wiggly larva hatched from each egg. Then nurse bees began to feed the larvae rich royal jelly so that they would grow into queen bees. After five and a half days, the nurses stopped feeding the larvae and sealed the cells with a cover of wax. After seven and a half days, a new queen cut open the little wax door of her cell and crawled out. The nurse bees stood around in awe and touched the new baby queen bee with their antennae and gave her food from their tongues. The new queen pushed the workers aside and rushed around, making angry, high-pitched piping sounds. And, holding up her mirror, this is what she screamed:

Who's the fairest of them all?
And suddenly she heard the mirror say,
'Snow White is prettier than you,
from now on you are number two.'
The queen said, 'Not so fast.
That little grub will not last.
I'll stab her with my sharp, sharp stinger,
I'll put her wings right through the wringer.'

The Queen went absolutely wild,
stabbing each new unborn child.
Outside they heard such a flutter
as each new grub was churned to butter.
The workers came to clean up the mess
(can't have this hive untidy,
even if it is Good Friday).
The Queen had fainted from the stress.

The west wind blew across a field of purple lavender, where the worker bees were busy gathering nectar for honey. It carried the sweet scent right into the dark woods. It filled the nostrils of Horace, who happened to be the mate of the unfortunate Bertha. He lifted up on his hind legs and sniffed some more.

"Bertha," he growled. "I smell Bertha." Bears have very sensitive noses, and his sense of smell was even stronger now because he wanted so much to see her. Horace emerged from the trees. His hair was heavy and his neck was drooped under its weight and it was a deep-blackish umber, so deep it turned purple in the sunlight. His bee-stung lips pouted. Then he noticed a strange sensation at his feet. Looking down, he saw a small green snake curling between his toes, almost nuzzling them, and trying to climb up his leg. He stamped his feet angrily to throw it off, not knowing that it was his beloved Bertha, who had been transformed into a snake by the Fairy Godmother. The pixies and water devas doubled up with laughter and clapped their tiny hands with glee as he went clumping along to the pond. But the bees just continued their work of gathering nectar from the sweet-smelling lavender. As fast as they filled their bee tummies, they flew back to the hive to pour it into the combs, and then flew back for more.

Soon the winking lights of the fireflies began to light up the field, and Horace headed to the pond for a drink. He plunged his big hairy brown feet into the warm ooze, where tiny translucent bodies of fish darted this way and that, each one reflecting the night sky like tiny mirrors. Just above the water, chrome green dragonflies hovered and zoomed like alien aircraft.

"Murf," he growled with pleasure, and bent over to stick his tongue in for a drink. He even slurped up some of the fish, and seemed to find them a bit chewy but quite tasty. Every now and then when he looked into the water, he saw a haunting reflection of Bertha. She seemed to be floating right below the surface. As he stared at this reflection, tears began to well up in his tiny black eyes and drip down his face. It was beyond belief to see this great big massive bear sit down and cry his heart out for his beloved mate. The fairies and water sprites saw it too and they all began to weep. And soon the level of the pond began to rise. It grew higher and higher, until it overflowed and started to flood the fields. The beavers spanked the water with their tails, alarmed at the prospect of a flood.

As the pond rose higher and higher, the crickets, who were playing a lovely concert on their violins, began floating around in the water, taking big gulps of water. They jumped onto the turtle's back, which became an oasis for them, and they took up their instruments again and continued to play, while water sprites encircled them in a dance of grief and mourning for the sad plight of Horace.

The next morning, as the sun rose in the sky, there was a great commotion in the hive. The queen was about to begin her flight. She took off like a golden rocket flying toward the sun. She flew so fast that the drones that flew after her were barely able to keep up. At last, one very strong and handsome drone caught up with her. They mated in the sky. They had fulfilled their purpose, and now she would return to the hive and lay thousands of eggs in the tiny combs that had been prepared for the bee nursery. A whole new generation of bees would be born and it would all start again. But for now they floated back to the hive to recover and sleep through the long cold winter.

Now, all of this did not go unnoticed. From behind her magic invisibility cape, Fairy Godmother watched all that was happening to Horace and the bees and the pond rising. She was profoundly touched by the deep love that Horace and Bertha shared, and so she decided to bring them together once again. Miraculously, the tiny green snake that Horace had almost tromped on reappeared, wriggling and slithering among the reeds. She looked up at Horace and flicked her forked tongue in a kind of welcoming smile. Horace cocked his head to one side and growled,

"Is that you, Bertha, my dearest darling?" She winked at him. Fairy Godmother waved her wand and suddenly a rainbow encircled the couple.
Bertha reappeared and Horace, overcome with joy and with tears rolling down his face, grabbed her with his big brown paws and gave her a bear hug that sent a thrill right down her spine. All the bees buzzed around them and brought them lovely bowls of the sweetest lavender honey, while Fairy Godmother hovered over them with her wand and offered a love blessing to the most loving couple in the woods.

HONEY-LOVING WAYS
Acknowledging DOO-WAH song ("Only the Lonely," by Roy Orbison)

REFERENCES:

FLIGHT OF THE HONEY BEE
By Raymond Huber
2013 Candlewick Press
Lib of Cong Cat # 2013931462
ISBB: 978-0-7636-6760-3

BEE
By Ting Morris
2005, Smart Apple Media
ISBN: 1-58340-378-7

A BEEKEEPER'S YEAR
By Sylvia A. Johnson
Little, Brown and Company (1994)
ISBN: 0-316-46745-6

HERE COME THE BEES!
By Alice E. Goudy
 Charles Scribner's Sons (1960)
Library of Congress Catalog Card # 60-6338

BEES
By Judith Jango-Cohen
Marshall Cavendish Benchmark (2007)
ISBN: 13: 978-0-7614-2235-8
         10: 0-7614-2235-8

www.ingramcontent.com/pod-product-compliance
Lightning Source LLC
Chambersburg PA
CBHW050927290526
45792CB00002B/920